The Life and Times

~ of the ~

ANT

Charles Micucci

Houghton Mifflin Company Boston 2003

An ant is a wise thing for itself,
but is a shrewd thing in an orchard or garden.
—Francis Bacon, 1561–1626

www.houghtonmifflinbooks.com

The text of this book is set in Stone Serif.
The illustrations are watercolor.

Library of Congress Cataloging-in-Publication Data
Micucci, Charles.
The life and times of the ant / by Charles Micucci.
p. cm.
Summary: Describes the evolution, physical characteristics, behavior, and social nature of ants.
ISBN 0-618-00559-5 (hardcover)
1. Ants—Juvenile literature. [1. Ants.] I. Title.
QL568.F7 M53 2003   595.79′6—dc21   2002000478

Manufactured in China
SCP 10 9 8 7 6 5 4 3 2 1

For Further Reading:

Goetsch, Wilhelm. *The Ants*. Ann Arbor: University of Michigan Press, 1957.
Hölldobler, Bert, and Edward O. Wilson. *Journey to the Ants*. Cambridge: Belknap Press of Harvard University Press, 1994.
Hoyt, Richard. *The Earth Dwellers*. New York: Simon and Schuster, 1996.
Hutchins, Ross E. *The Ant Realm*. New York: Dodd, Mead, 1967.
Ordish, George. *The Year of the Ant*. New York: Charles Scribner's Sons, 1978.
Wheeler, William M. *Ants: Their Structure, Development, and Behavior*. New York: Columbia University Press, 1910.

Contents

Masters of the Earth

Ants have been digging through dirt for more than 100 million years. Their dynasty stretches from the time of dinosaurs to today.

They are one of the world's most important insects. They plow more soil than beetles, eat more bugs than praying mantises, and outnumber many insects by 7 million to 1.

Tunneling out of jungles and forests and into back yards on every continent except Antarctica, ants ramble on as if they own the Earth. Perhaps they do.

GREAT DYNASTIES ON EARTH

100,000,000 B.C.   65,000,000 B.C.   TODAY

PEOPLE

ANTS

DINOSAURS

WORKING

Ounce for ounce, an ant is one of the strongest animals on earth. An ant can lift a seed five times its weight, while an elephant can lift a log only one fifth of its weight.

Each year, the world's ants dig up more than 16 billion tons of dirt—enough to fill 3 billion dump trucks.

Ants are frequently compared with people because they live in social communities and work together to solve their problems.

Friends in Low Places

There are more than a million kinds of insects. Most of them are solitary insects. Their survival depends on only one being—themselves.

An ant is different; it is a social insect. It cannot survive by itself for long periods of time. Ants need other ants to help build a nest, gather food, and protect themselves from enemies. This need for other ants is not a weakness but a strength that enables the ant to overcome its small size.

When an ant is threatened by a larger insect, it emits a scent called an alarm pheromone. Other ants smell the odor and rush to help.

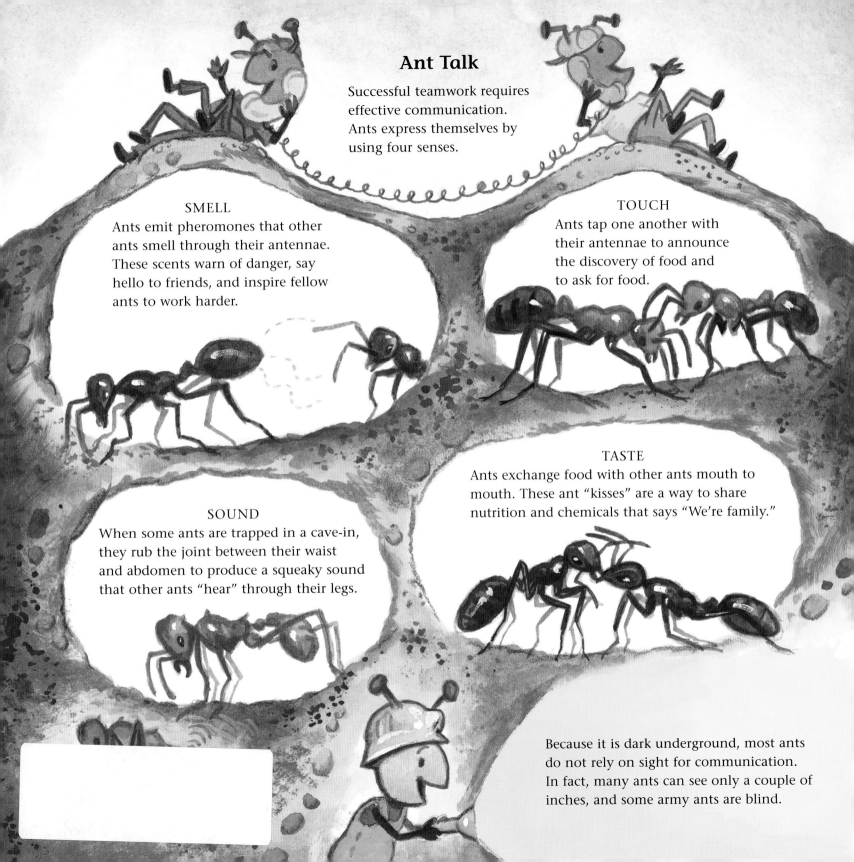

Ant Talk

Successful teamwork requires effective communication. Ants express themselves by using four senses.

SMELL

Ants emit pheromones that other ants smell through their antennae. These scents warn of danger, say hello to friends, and inspire fellow ants to work harder.

TOUCH

Ants tap one another with their antennae to announce the discovery of food and to ask for food.

TASTE

Ants exchange food with other ants mouth to mouth. These ant "kisses" are a way to share nutrition and chemicals that says "We're family."

SOUND

When some ants are trapped in a cave-in, they rub the joint between their waist and abdomen to produce a squeaky sound that other ants "hear" through their legs.

Because it is dark underground, most ants do not rely on sight for communication. In fact, many ants can see only a couple of inches, and some army ants are blind.

The Ant Family

Ants live in social groups called colonies. A small colony may contain only 12 ants, while a large colony overflows with more than 7 million ants. Each colony has three types of ants: workers, male ants, and the queen ant.

WORKER ANTS

Most of the colony's ants are workers. They are all female, but they do not lay eggs. Although they are the smallest ants, they do all of the chores: clean the nest, gather food, and defend the colony. When you see an ant dragging a crumb of food, you are looking at a worker.

MALE ANTS

All males have wings and can be seen for only a few weeks in the summer. They mate with the queen but do no work in the colony.

QUEEN ANT

The queen ant lays eggs and is the mother of all the ants. Young queens have wings, but old queens do not. All queens have large abdomens to produce eggs. Some queens lay millions of eggs per year.

How an Ant Colony Starts

After a hot summer rain, a young queen takes off on her mating flight. The queen flies into a cloud of male ants and mates in the air.

Afterward, all the males die, and the queen returns to the earth. She breaks her wings off by rubbing them on the ground.

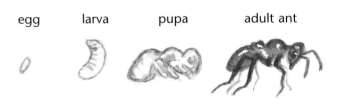

egg   larva   pupa   adult ant

Then she digs a hole in the soft, moist earth and starts laying eggs. She will never leave the nest again.

During the next three months, the eggs develop through four stages: egg, larva, pupa, and adult ant.

After they have hatched, the first workers assume the duties of the colony. They search for food and protect the queen. As the queen lays more eggs, the workers enlarge the nest.

Inside an Anthill

Most ants build their homes underground. Ants dig by scooping dirt with their mandibles (jaws). As they chew the dirt, it mixes with their saliva to form little bricks. Then they pack the little bricks together to reinforce the tunnels. Finally, the ants carry the excess dirt outside with their mandibles, and it gradually forms an anthill.

Beneath the anthill lies the ant nest. Small nests have only one chamber just inches below the surface, while large nests may have thousands of chambers and may be as deep as twenty feet. All nests provide shelter from the weather and a safe environment for the queen ant to lay eggs.

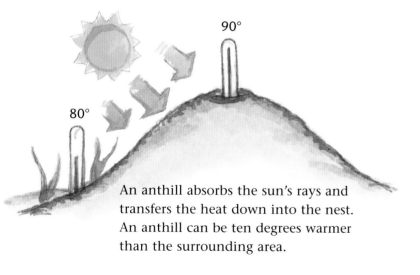

90°

80°

An anthill absorbs the sun's rays and transfers the heat down into the nest. An anthill can be ten degrees warmer than the surrounding area.

Ants often nest beneath a rock or log, which protects the nest and traps moisture in the dirt. Ants require moisture so that their bodies do not dry out.

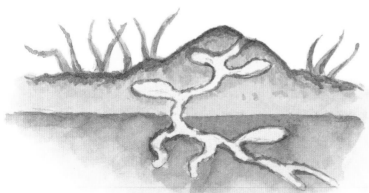

Ants dig their nests deep enough to reach damp dirt. As air dries out the nest, they dig new tunnels into the damp dirt.

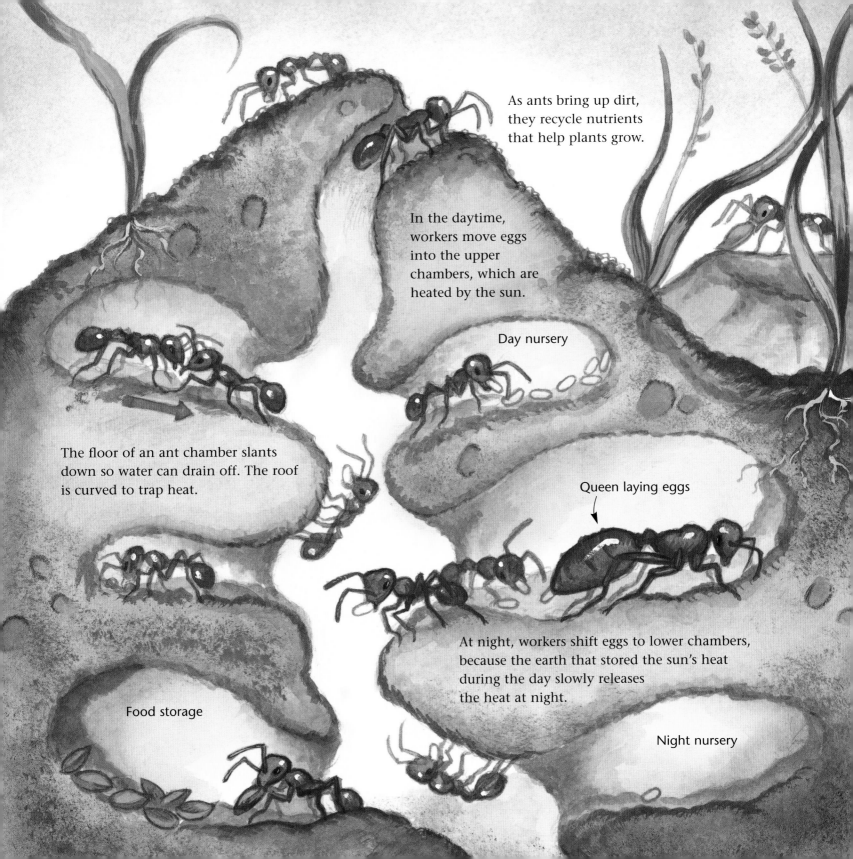

As ants bring up dirt, they recycle nutrients that help plants grow.

In the daytime, workers move eggs into the upper chambers, which are heated by the sun.

Day nursery

The floor of an ant chamber slants down so water can drain off. The roof is curved to trap heat.

Queen laying eggs

At night, workers shift eggs to lower chambers, because the earth that stored the sun's heat during the day slowly releases the heat at night.

Food storage

Night nursery

House Plants

Many ants that do not live underground live in plants. Often, the plant and the ants benefit each other. The plant shelters the ants' nest. In return, the ants protect the plant from predators, add nutrients to the plant, or pollinate the plant so new plants will grow.

Ants live in all parts of plants, including the flowers, seeds, leaves, thorns, branches, and trunk. In the South American rain forest, a single tree may house more than seventy kinds of ants.

FLOWERS
In the rain forest, ants live in orchids that hang from trees. The ants carry nutrients from the jungle floor up to the orchids.

SEEDS
Beneath mighty oak trees lives the small acorn ant. Up to a hundred ants may live in each acorn.

LEAVES

Weaver ants use their larvae, which spin silk cocoons, as sewing machines to bind their nests.

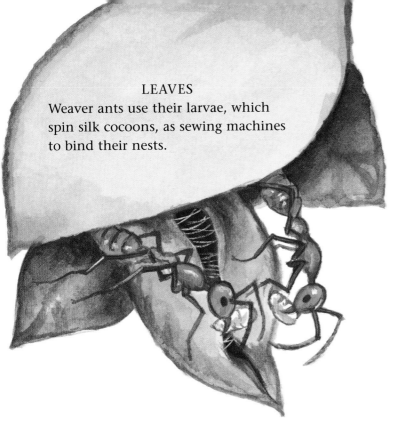

THORNS

Acacia ants live in the thorns of the acacia tree. Patrolling the tree night and day, the ants sting all intruders and clear weeds away from the trunk.

BRANCHES

Trap-door ants have special workers with flat heads called soldiers. They block the nest entrance with their head to prevent enemies from entering.

TRUNKS

Carpenter ants build nests by carving out tree trunks. Their nests may stretch for thirty feet inside the tree.

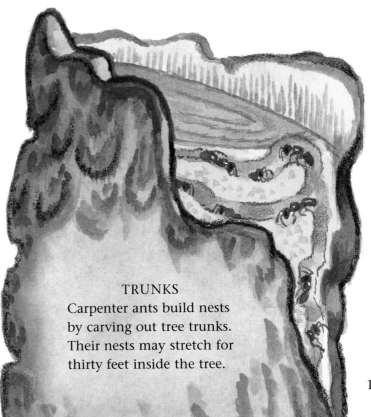

The Ant's Body

Most ants are between ¹⁄₁₆ and ½ inch long. Together, nine hundred of them would weigh less than an ounce. Despite their small size, the world's ants move tons of dirt and capture millions of insects each day.

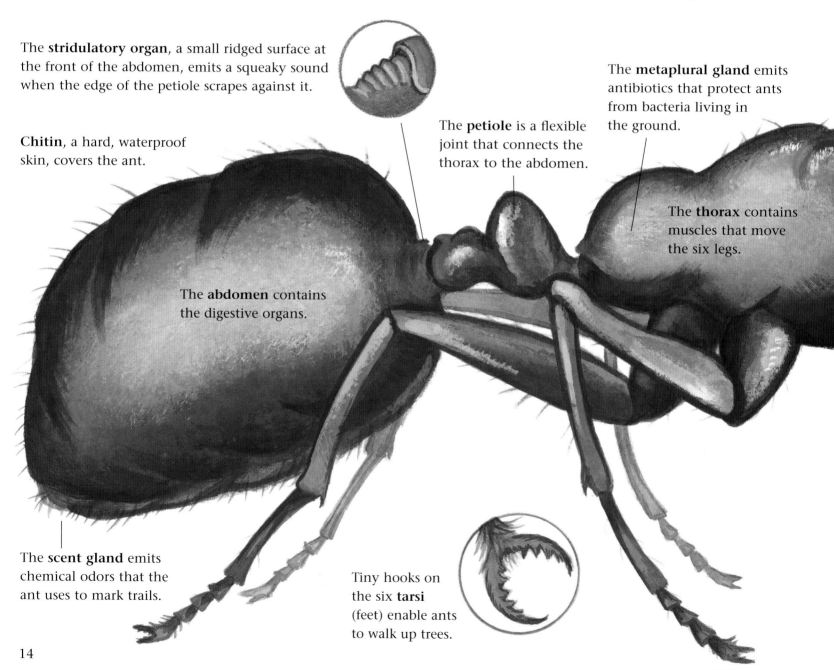

The **stridulatory organ**, a small ridged surface at the front of the abdomen, emits a squeaky sound when the edge of the petiole scrapes against it.

Chitin, a hard, waterproof skin, covers the ant.

The **petiole** is a flexible joint that connects the thorax to the abdomen.

The **metaplural gland** emits antibiotics that protect ants from bacteria living in the ground.

The **thorax** contains muscles that move the six legs.

The **abdomen** contains the digestive organs.

The **scent gland** emits chemical odors that the ant uses to mark trails.

Tiny hooks on the six **tarsi** (feet) enable ants to walk up trees.

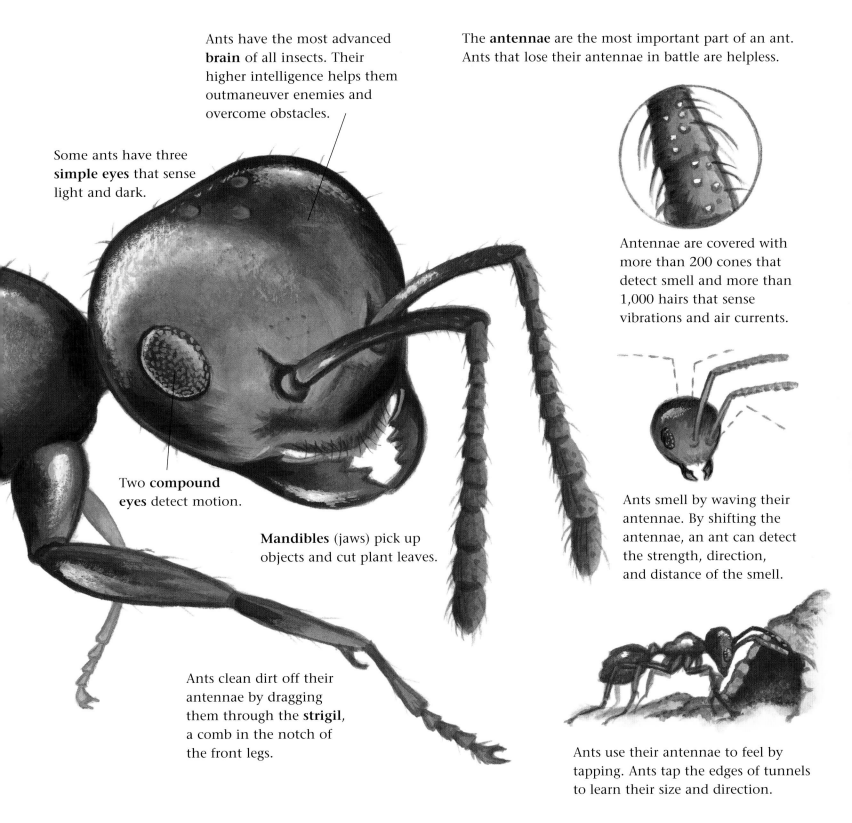

Ants have the most advanced **brain** of all insects. Their higher intelligence helps them outmaneuver enemies and overcome obstacles.

The **antennae** are the most important part of an ant. Ants that lose their antennae in battle are helpless.

Some ants have three **simple eyes** that sense light and dark.

Antennae are covered with more than 200 cones that detect smell and more than 1,000 hairs that sense vibrations and air currents.

Two **compound eyes** detect motion.

Mandibles (jaws) pick up objects and cut plant leaves.

Ants smell by waving their antennae. By shifting the antennae, an ant can detect the strength, direction, and distance of the smell.

Ants clean dirt off their antennae by dragging them through the **strigil**, a comb in the notch of the front legs.

Ants use their antennae to feel by tapping. Ants tap the edges of tunnels to learn their size and direction.

A Life of Work

Ants begin their working lives by cleaning themselves. In a couple of days they start sharing food and licking each other. These food exchanges bond the colony together. There is no boss ant, but active ants usually begin doing chores and then other ants join in.

Younger ants work in the nest—tending the queen ant, feeding larvae, and digging tunnels. After a couple of months, the ants leave the nest to search for food. There is no retirement; worn out or battle-scarred, ants work until they die.

QUEEN TENDER
Young ants help the queen deliver her eggs by grabbing the eggs with their mandibles.

NURSE ANT
Ants lick larvae so they do not dry out, and feed them so they grow.

FORAGERS

The oldest ants search for food. Most foragers search within fifty feet of the nest, but if food is scarce, they may travel thousands of feet.

GUARD

When ants first leave the nest, they stand near the entrance, blocking strange ants from entering.

TUNNEL DIGGER

As the population grows, ants dig more tunnels for the increased traffic and new chambers to store the eggs and larvae.

Digging holes can be hard work. To remove a pile of dirt 6 inches high, 6 inches wide, and 6 inches long requires 500,000 loads of dirt.

6

5

4

3

2

1

Show Me the Way

Every warm day, foraging ants patrol the colony's territory. They are not just wandering; they are searching for food. When an ant finds food, she rushes back to the colony while laying a scent trail. It is the scent trail that leads the other ants to the food source.

Each forager moves out in a different direction. One of the ants discovers a cookie crumb. She investigates it with her antennae. Then she tries to drag it home, but it's too big.

So she rushes home to get help. Every couple of steps she bumps her abdomen against the ground and her scent gland releases an invisible vapor, which forms a scent trail.

Back inside the colony, the forager alerts other ants about the cookie by tapping them with her antennae. Suddenly, several ants rush out and follow the scent trail to the food.

Each of the new ants harvests part of the cookie and transports it back to the colony while laying a scent trail of her own.

Soon the vapors of the scent trail are so thick that many more ants join the harvest. As they return, the foraging ants share their feast with the ants inside the nest. Within twenty-four hours, every ant in the colony has tasted the cookie.

Grass Root Highways

Some ants connect their anthills to food sources by a system of ant trails. Unlike scent trails, which are invisible, these trails can be easily seen. Construction crews remove grass and twigs to form paths two to six inches wide that may stretch over six hundred feet. When food is plentiful, a thousand ants per foot crowd the trail. Established ant colonies may travel over the same grass root highways for many years.

In forests, wood ants connect their anthills together by ant trails. Large wood ant colonies transport thousands of caterpillars and insects a day over their trails.

Harvester ants construct their trails to wildflowers, where they collect seeds. Surrounding their anthills, discarded seeds sprout into new plants.

Some ant trails are so well preserved that larger animals such as deer and even people may use them as footpaths.

GRASS ROOT BRIDGES

Army ants form living bridges to cross streams by linking themselves together.

GRASS ROOT TUNNELS

Many kinds of ants dig tunnels under streams and other obstacles. Leafcutter ants can dig tunnels five hundred feet long, which may bypass several streams.

GRASS ROOT SPEED LIMITS

Harlow Shapley, an astronomer whose hobby was ants, tested their speed. He discovered that they run faster on hot days.

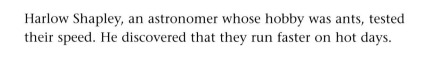

TEMPERATURE	78°F	85°F	92°F
SPEED* (inches per second)	1	1⅜	1⅝

*Speeds are for the Argentine ant

An Ant Calendar

Most insects and male ants live only a couple of months, but workers and queen ants live longer. Workers may live more than four years, and queens fifteen years. Working together, ants prepare for the different seasons.

FEBRUARY
When the temperature is about 50 degrees, ants repair the nest and search for food.

MARCH
As the weather warms and food becomes more plentiful, the old queen begins laying eggs.

JUNE
The young queens and males fill the sky to mate. Then the young queens fly off to start a new colony, while the old queen stays in the nest.

JULY
Picnic season is a busy time for ants. A colony of ants can devour a cookie in less than a half-hour.

OCTOBER
The queen lays her last eggs, which are eaten by the worker ants so they will survive the winter.

NOVEMBER
Ants winterize their home by plugging up the holes.

APRIL–MAY
Ants collect honeydew (a sweet liquid) from aphids.

Aphids feed on plants and convert the plant juices into honeydew.

When an ant strokes the aphid with her antennae...

the aphid releases a drop of honeydew, which the ant eats.

AUGUST
Throughout the summer some ants may work all day and through the night collecting food for the colony.

SEPTEMBER
As summer food sources decline, ants wage war to capture food and ant eggs.

Each year, ants live and die, but the colony goes on. Some colonies live in the same nest for eighty years or more.

DECEMBER–JANUARY
Three feet underground (below the frost line), the colony huddles around the queen to stay warm.

Kinds of Ants

There are about 10,000 kinds of ants. Myrmecologists—scientists who study ants—believe there are thousands more yet to be discovered. Although all ants are similar, each kind of ant has distinct traits that enable it to exist in its unique environment.

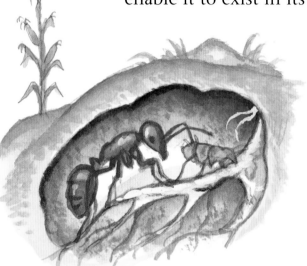

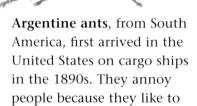

Cornfield ants are the most plentiful ants in the United States. They live under sidewalks and in meadows and cornfields. They raise aphids for honeydew.

Little black ants are common in back yards and gardens. They eat honeydew from aphids and food crumbs.

Argentine ants, from South America, first arrived in the United States on cargo ships in the 1890s. They annoy people because they like to live in houses.

Fire ants sting many people each year. They are a pest in southern states because they damage farm crops.

Acrobat ants often walk with their abdomens tilted up. They raise aphids and other insects in their ant-garden homes.

Carpenter ants live in logs and old wood. They do not eat wood, but dig tunnels through wood for their nests.

Wood ants live in six-foot-high anthills made of dirt and pine needles. They protect forests by removing insects that damage trees.

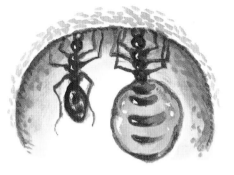

Honeypot ants live in deserts, where they collect nectar and sap from plants. Special workers called repletes serve as living storage containers for their honey.

Harvester ants collect seeds for food. They dig their large anthills, sometimes ten feet in diameter, in deserts and prairies.

Weaver ants live hundreds of feet up in the treetops of Africa, Asia, and Australia. They chase other ants, animals, and birds from their trees.

Leafcutter ants saw leaves from plants so fast that a colony can strip a tree overnight. A large colony can have a population of 7 million ants.

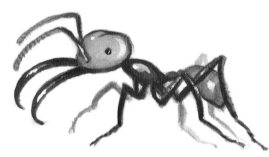

Army ants are among the most feared jungle insects. Marching in long columns, they eat every animal they find, from scorpions to pythons.

Bulldog ants are the fiercest ants of Australia. More than one inch long, with saw-toothed jaws, they can jump a foot or more.

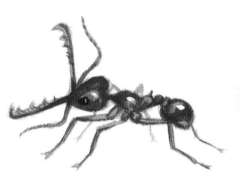

Trap-jaw ants can shut their wide jaws in less than one-thousandth of a second, faster than any other animal.

Each year, **myrmecologists** travel around the world and peek into many hiding places to find new kinds of ants.

Recycling the Rain Forest

CANOPY
100 feet

UNDERSTORY
1–99 feet

Ants live in
all four layers
of the forest.
Most animals
live in only
one or two.

FOREST FLOOR

UNDERGROUND

The rain forest is home to millions of animals. Each one plays a vital role there, but perhaps the most important tasks are done by one of the smallest animals, the ant.

Inch by inch, ants patrol every corner of the rain forest. They eat insect pests, remove decaying animals from the forest floor, plant gardens in trees, and thin out plants that overcrowd the forest.

A column of army ants can attack thirty thousand insect pests each day. This prevents maggots and roaches from overpopulating the rain forest.

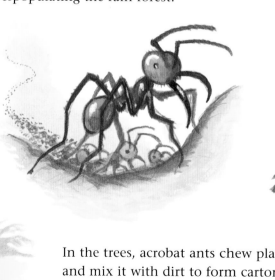

In the trees, acrobat ants chew plant fiber and mix it with dirt to form carton nests. Then they plant seeds in the carton. When it rains, vines and other plants grow.

How Ants Recycle Leaves

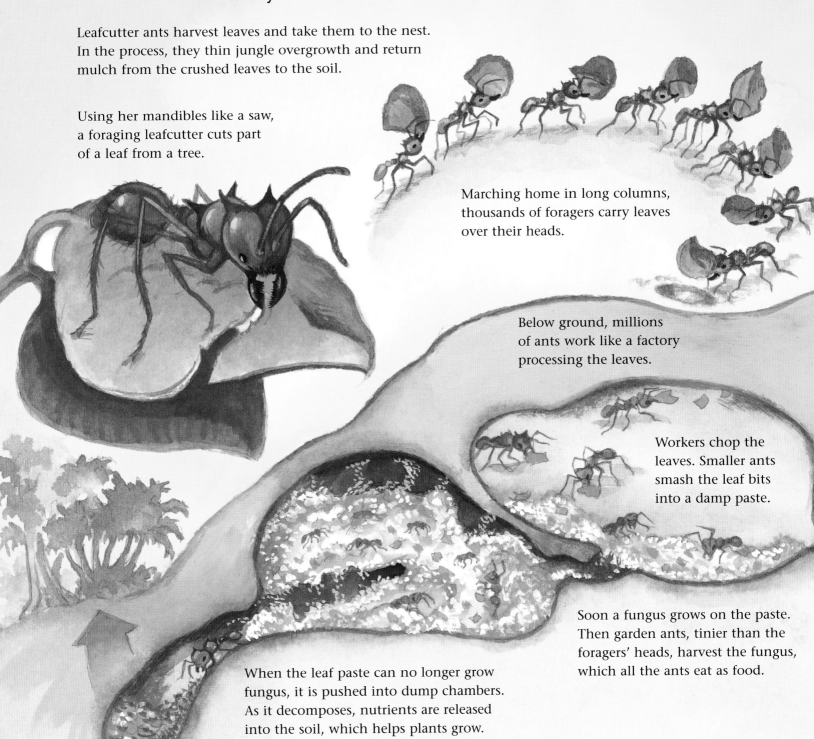

Leafcutter ants harvest leaves and take them to the nest. In the process, they thin jungle overgrowth and return mulch from the crushed leaves to the soil.

Using her mandibles like a saw, a foraging leafcutter cuts part of a leaf from a tree.

Marching home in long columns, thousands of foragers carry leaves over their heads.

Below ground, millions of ants work like a factory processing the leaves.

Workers chop the leaves. Smaller ants smash the leaf bits into a damp paste.

Soon a fungus grows on the paste. Then garden ants, tinier than the foragers' heads, harvest the fungus, which all the ants eat as food.

When the leaf paste can no longer grow fungus, it is pushed into dump chambers. As it decomposes, nutrients are released into the soil, which helps plants grow.

woodpecker

horned lizard

armadillo

A Dangerous World

When you are only a quarter-inch tall, the world can be a dangerous place. Every time an ant leaves home, there is a risk that she will not return. Horned lizards lap up ants as they exit the nest, woodpeckers pick them off as they climb trees, and ant lions ambush them in sand pits.

Sometimes ants are not safe even in their own homes. Armadillos feast on burrowing ants, as does the biggest home wrecker of all: the giant anteater of Central and South America. Seven feet long and weighing as much as seventy pounds, a giant anteater can tear open an ant nest in minutes and devour twenty thousand ants in one meal.

Sand Trap of No Return

The ant lion digs a circular sand pit and waits at the bottom.

When an ant looks into the pit, the ant lion tosses sand into the air to trip up the ant.

The ant stumbles into the pit, and the ant lion grabs it with its large pincers.

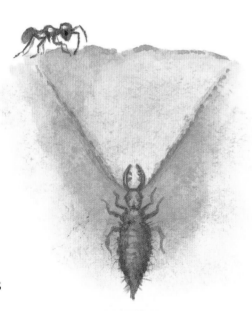

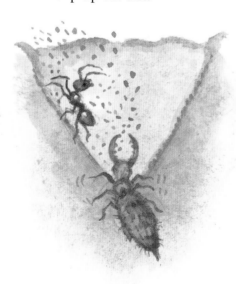

The Giant Anteater

The giant anteater is a slow, nearsighted, toothless animal that has escaped extinction for one reason only: it specializes in eating ants and termites.

Thick bristles of **hair** protect the body from insect stings.

The **stomach** wall absorbs ant stings and has special muscles that crush ants so they can be digested.

The long **snout** drives deep into the nest. Anteaters use their strong sense of smell to locate ants.

Four-inch **claws** can dig through hard dirt or tree trunks.

A three-foot-long **tail** with fifteen-inch hairs sweeps up escaping ants.

The **mouth** opens only a quarter-inch, about the width of a pencil.

The wormlike **tongue** stretches nineteen inches beyond the mouth. The tongue is coated with gluey saliva, which causes ants to stick to it.

Tunneling Through Time

Ants evolved from wasps more than 100 million years ago. They have been dodging footsteps ever since. As dinosaurs thundered above ground, ants dug out a home below. The mighty dinosaurs are long gone, but the little ant has survived.

Today, myrmecologists search for the secrets of the ants' long existence and how those traits may benefit our society. They study ant fossils in prehistoric amber and observe the daily habits of ant colonies.

100,000,000 B.C. Ants dug tunnels under dinosaurs.

90,000,000 B.C. Two ants were sealed in amber. Millions of years later, the amber was found in New Jersey.

65,000,000 B.C. Some scientists think a giant meteorite crashed into Earth, killing the dinosaurs. But ants, which could hide underground, survived the disaster.

2000 B.C. Aborigines in Australia ate the honey of honeypot ants. Their modern descendants call these sweet ants *yarumpa*.

400 B.C. Herodotus, a Greek historian, wrote about ants that mined gold. Today, some miners sift through anthills to learn what minerals lie underground.

1500s–1800s When Europeans conquered the Caribbean islands, their forts were frequently invaded by ants. They offered rewards and prayed to Saint Saturnin to stop the six-legged armies.

A.D. 1200–1300 Chinese farmers used ants to keep their orange trees free of insect pests.

How Amber Is Formed

Millions of years ago, an ant walks on a tree.

Tree sap drips onto the ant. As the sap dries in the air, it hardens.

Years pass, and the tree washes out to sea. Tossed by the waves, the hardened sap sinks to the bottom.

Tides wash the hardened sap against the shore, where it becomes polished amber.

1687 Anton van Leeuwenhoek, who invented the microscope, discovered ant eggs and pupae.

DO NOT DISTURB ANT NESTS

1890s–1930s William Wheeler, one of America's first myrmecologists, traveled around the world collecting ants and ant fossils.

1880 Germany passed a law protecting wood ants because they kept trees free of pests.

1991 Bert Hölldobler and Edward O. Wilson, two myrmecologists, won the Pulitzer Prize for their book *The Ants*.

1859 The biologist Charles Darwin wrote about ant intelligence and teamwork in his classic work *The Origin of Species*.

2000 Scientists applied ant behavior as a model for computer networks. Computer systems based on ant behavior re-routed around problems quicker than previous systems did.

The tunnel of time continues for the ants. Their hard work inspires people today, as it has for many centuries. Look down on a warm day and you will probably find an ant. Drop a piece of food...and an ant will probably find you.

Inspired by ants' labor, Aesop (sixth century B.C.) wrote the fable "The Ant and the Grasshopper."

During the summer, the ant gathered food while the lazy grasshopper sang a song.

When winter arrived, the ant had food, but the grasshopper had none.

Moral: Work hard today so you are prepared for tomorrow.

Ants have been admired in Asia for over a thousand years. In Japanese brush script, the symbol for "ant" combines "insect" with "unselfishness," "justice," and "courtesy."

To inspire his people, King Solomon, a great leader of ancient Israel, said: "Go to the ant...consider her ways and be wise."

DATE DUE

MEDIALOG INC
Butler, KY 41006

Selection
Junior Library Guild